WEBSTER FAMILY STORIES

Judith Young

**Illustrations by
Erika Diaz**

TEACH Services, Inc.
PUBLISHING
www.TEACHServices.com • (800) 367-1844

World rights reserved. This book or any portion thereof may not be copied or reproduced in any form or manner whatever, except as provided by law, without the written permission of the publisher, except by a reviewer who may quote brief passages in a review.

The author assumes full responsibility for the accuracy of all facts and quotations as cited in this book. The opinions expressed in this book are the author's personal views and interpretations, and do not necessarily reflect those of the publisher.

This book is provided with the understanding that the publisher is not engaged in giving spiritual, legal, medical, or other professional advice. If authoritative advice is needed, the reader should seek the counsel of a competent professional.

_____

Copyright © 2018 Judith Young
Copyright © 2018 TEACH Services, Inc.
ISBN-13: 978-1-4796-0917-8 (Paperback)
ISBN-13: 978-1-4796-0918-5 (ePub)
Library of Congress Control Number: 2018950322

TEACH Services, Inc.
PUBLISHING
www.TEACHServices.com • (800) 367-1844

ACKNOWLEDGMENTS

My deepest sense of thankfulness and gratitude:

– to my son Justin Young

– to Larry and to each of our children for their support

– to Erika for all the beautiful illustrations

– to all my friends for their encouragements

DEDICATION

I dedicate this book to you:

– to all my sisters and brothers for all their input and help, I love you

– to all my grandchildren, nieces, and nephews

– in honor of my father

– to the loving memory of my mother Dorothy Webster

TABLE OF CONTENTS

THE HORSE REFUSES TO MOVE 7

SNAKE ON THE PORCH 9

THE STORM 11

THE PAPAYA TREE MIRACLE 13

A STILL, SMALL VOICE—*By Grandpa Joseph* 15

LEARNING TO SWIM—*By Atherine, Judith, and Rachel* 17

THE HURRICANE 19

MY FIRST EARTHQUAKE EXPERIENCE—*By My Brother, Ledly Webster* 21

ROSITA, THE PET CHICKEN—*By My Brother, Duane Webster* 23

MY FIRST DAY OF SCHOOL—*By My Brother, Jerry Webster* 25

HOW DO I KNOW?—*By My Sister, Esther Webster Wills* 27

THE HORSE REFUSES TO MOVE

On a sunny Sabbath, Saturday evening, we were on our way to tell Bible stories to the kids on the other side of the island.

Dad said, "Girls, let's go!"

My dad Joseph, my sisters Atherine, Rachel, Esther, and I (Judith) all got on our grandfather's horse and started crossing the island of Roatan, Honduras. About halfway the clip, clop … "Oh! No!" The horse stopped suddenly and refused to move. We all got off the horse. We tried pulling the horse, but he would not move. We walked him backwards and he moved; we tried to go forward, but he refused!

"What is wrong with the horse, Dad?" we asked.

Dad tried again. Forward—nothing, backward—yes.

Dad said, "He sees a spirit on the path!"

"Ooohhh, no!" We all got scared. Dad took his handkerchief, covered the horse's eyes, and then walked the horse forward a few feet. Then he took the handkerchief off. We all got back on the horse and made it to the other side where the children and their parents were waiting for us to sing and Dad to tell the Bible stories about Jesus.

SNAKE ON THE PORCH

It was a Sunday morning; Dad was chopping some bushes and cutting the grass around the house. As he continued to chop, he looked up, and suddenly a huge snake was right in front of him. "Ohh, my goodness!!!" We ran to see what was wrong and saw Dad dragging the snake across the front of the yard on a pile of dry brush. The snake was now dead.

Dad told us that this type of snake travels in pairs. He said his mate would come looking for him. About five days later the female snake came looking. She followed the scent of the other snake. We were sitting on the porch, and I decided to look up. "Ooh, no!!" I was speechless. The six-foot-plus snake was curled around the top of the porch just looking at us.

We ran and got Mother, who came to our rescue! She had a machete in her hand, caught the snake, and took it off the porch to the pile of dry bushes. That snake also died that day. Mom was not afraid to get that snake to protect her children from harm. We never saw another snake on our porch again. Jesus protected our family from being harmed by snakes.

THE STORM

It was a summer Sunday morning about 6:00 a.m. Dad came to our room and said, "Girls, wake up, we are going fishing."

We jumped out of bed, happy to go. My sister, Atherine, and I got dressed, and we were ready to go and fish. We would have fresh fried snappers for dinner that day! We got in the canoe and set out on our fish hunt. We each had our own set of paddles to help steer the canoe. We ended up crossing the reef into the deep blue sea. We traveled about five miles to an area called Dixon Cove. Then we started throwing our lines out to catch some delicious fish. I caught one, my sister caught one, and my dad caught one too!

My dad suddenly started yelling, "Girls, we need to start leaving for home!"

"Why? We are just getting started, Dad!"

My dad then pointed to the skies above us.

"Look at the dark clouds!"

A storm slowly started to cover the bright blue sky. We quickly pulled our fishing lines into the boat, and we started to paddle as fast as we could. The clouds were moving closer and closer toward us. We had no time to get home before the rain started beating down on us. We finally made it to the beach and ran for cover under some huge fifty-year-old mango trees. We were at the mango grove! Those huge trees saved us from being beaten by the heavy rain. Wet, shivering, tired, and cold, we waited out the heavy part of the storm for more than thirty minutes almost hugging the mango tree. It was like a huge umbrella that provided shelter from the heavy rain.

The rain finally stopped, and we got back into our canoe and started for home. We stayed close to the beach all the way until we got to town, then finally home. We later enjoyed the delicious supper that Mom prepared with the fried red snappers. Later that evening at family worship we gave Jesus thanks for protecting us from the storm.

THE PAPAYA TREE MIRACLE

It was the beginning of a new year when every family at church would pledge something to Jesus for the Investment Offering. Some families would have bake sales, other families would pledge money every month for the entire year for investment to Jesus. My family was large and didn't have a lot of money, so we had a family talk and decided to dedicate one of the four papaya trees in front of our house for Investment to Jesus. Every fruit that the tree bore we would sell and give the money to the church for Investment to help other boys and girls in other parts of the world to learn about Jesus.

The papaya trees started getting taller, and flowers came out. Then the little papayas came out and started getting bigger and bigger and bigger. Ooh, my goodness! The tree was loaded with big watermelon-sized papayas. Dad had to prop the trees up with sticks to prevent them from breaking. The papayas were all green on the trees when a hurricane hit the island. It rained, and the wind blew all night. The storm was finally over.

The next morning three of the papaya trees had blown down, except the one we had dedicated to Jesus. Wow! Not one papaya had fallen off the investment tree after a big hurricane. Our parents bought some of the papayas for our family, and we sold all the rest to friends and neighbors. God protected that tree through a hurricane! It pays to dedicate everything to Jesus!

A STILL, SMALL VOICE
—*By Grandpa Joseph*

The shipping company called Dad to go and relieve the cook while he went on vacation. Dad traveled to the airport, and then a still, small voice said, "Go back home, Joseph!"

He obeyed and went back home. Dad called and told them that he changed his mind about coming to work. They got mad and told him he would not be able to work anymore with the company.

I started crying and said, "God will provide."

Later on, Captain Paul hired Dad on his ship from Roatan Island to Miami, Florida, USA. Dad learned later on that Captain Paul was in port on the day that the company fired him.

Dad also found out that a week later the ship was on fire and some of the men jumped overboard, and some of them drowned. "Ooooh!" He was so thankful to God and thankful that he listened to the still, small voice of the Holy Spirit that day.

LEARNING TO SWIM
—By Atherine, Judith, and Rachel

While living on Roatan Island, Honduras, Dad would wake us up early in the morning before going to school to teach us to swim. He would take us on the wharf, throw us in the water, and say, "Swim!"

After we swallowed a little water, he would jump in, hold us, and teach us how to move our hands and feet in the water. He then took us back up on the wharf, threw us in, and said, "Swim! Swim!"

We started swimming like puppies and stayed floating. That is how he taught us to swim. Later on, we were very good. We swam across the deep to the barrier reef and back to the shore. We learned to listen and obey what he told us to do.

THE HURRICANE

The radio station announced that a hurricane was headed for Puerto Cortes, Honduras. The eye of the hurricane was expected to hit our town in two days. They also announced that anyone living on the waterfront must move to higher grounds. Our home was also on the waterfront.

Mother said that we must all pack our clothes to have enough for five days. We would leave for San Pedro Sula, about seventy-five kilometers away, to our aunt Leah's home. We also packed some groceries for the trip. Early the next morning we went to the bus station and got on the bus to San Pedro. We arrived two hours later, settled in with our aunt, and waited out the hurricane.

It was raining all day and night, and some neighborhoods were flooded. After the hurricane was over, we returned home to find a huge barge full of red beans in our backyard. Our neighbor told us that all our other neighbors stood watching the scary scene of this huge barge coming directly toward our home.

When we first moved there, my father had a fence of large conch shells built in the water around the back of our home to protect our home from anything that drifted by. Our home was mostly over the water. Only the front porch and steps were on land. Well, it paid off that day.

The wind and the waves pushed the barge directly toward our home. But the neighbors and all the spectators watching to see our home destroyed by the barge were surprised when the huge barge stopped right on all the hundreds of conch shells that father had used to build a fence around the back of our home for protection. We prayed before we left home that evening in our family worship for God to protect our home from the terrible hurricane. Many homes in our neighborhood were destroyed and blown away. We thanked Jesus for His protection in saving our home from being destroyed.

MY FIRST EARTHQUAKE EXPERIENCE
—*By My Brother, Ledly Webster*

It was early in the morning just before sunlight, when it happened. The house started shaking and rocking back and forth. It was an earthquake! We all started screaming and calling each other. We all ran to the front door at the same time. "Ooooh no!" We are all jammed in the doorway together.

The shaking stopped and my sister, Esther, then stooped down and crawled between our legs and got out first. We then got loose and ran outside. We had started going toward our neighbor's home when I saw the swamp area beside our home bubbling from the earth like a pot of boiling water. The sun was now shining, and for the first time I saw a huge crack in the street. Wow!

The earthquake made several cracks in the street. All I could do was stare in shock and fear, as I looked around and saw our neighbor's house had fallen off its posts. When we finally got back to our house, we realized it was tilted down at the back. The post had fallen from the back part of our house. Later on, Father had the post replaced. Nothing was damaged inside of our home that day. We realized that God had spared us from a major disaster. The entire port of Cortes was damaged.

ROSITA, THE PET CHICKEN
—By My Brother, Duane Webster

One day while playing in the house, we heard our chickens running and making a lot of noise.

Mom said, "Go and see what is going on with the chickens."

I ran outside and saw my sister's favorite hen , Rosita, being dragged under the fence by a large opossum. I ran and got the broomstick and started hitting the opossum on the head until he let her go. The opossum started growling at me and grabbed the chicken again. I hit the opossum several times until he let Rosita loose.

Poor Rosita! She was our favorite hen. Sometimes we would sneak her into our room and play with her. On that day the opossum hurt her wings, and her leg was chewed up, but she survived that opossum attack. The next day we came back from school and Mother told us that it was best to cook Rosita for dinner that evening.

It was the custom that all families raise chickens to eat. We all sat at the dinner table staring at our plates, and no one could eat her—not even Mom—except our favorite cousin, Steve, that was staying with us. He started smiling because he had our share to eat. Eating one's pet was not something we were prepared to do.

MY FIRST DAY OF SCHOOL
—By My Brother, Jerry Webster

I was five years old, and the day I was waiting for had finally arrived. I was ready to go to school. I had my backpack, my pencil, and my notebook. I was ready. I asked Mom to wake me up early the next morning to be ready. I went to sleep with excitement.

I woke up early the next morning, Mom made a delicious porridge, and I got dressed. We had our family devotion, and my sisters, Rachel and Esther, were walking me to school following Mom's instruction. As we walked, and I realized I was going to kindergarten, I started crying and walking. My crying got so loud the neighbors looked out to see what was going on.

They immediately grabbed me firmly by the arms, one on each arm. Then I started to pull back trying to return home. At one point they let me go and started walking on the other side of the street, trying not to identify with me because of the tantrum I was making. When I turned back heading for home, that is when they grabbed ahold of me and dragged me to school.

When we got there and I saw the other children, I calmed down, and my sisters left for home walking as fast as they could. Our little brother, Jerry's, first day of school was memorable!

HOW DO I KNOW?
—By My Sister, Esther Webster Wills

It was the summer of 1980. I was eighteen years old when my family migrated to Corozal, Belize, Central America. The first week our family went to church, my sister, Rachel, and I were looking around at everyone in church and feeling out of place when two young men got up to sing the special music. Philip played the guitar, and Herman sang the solo for the service. I leaned over to my sister and said, "Herman is mine."

She whispered back and said, "The tall one is mine."

It was just a passing comment. Weeks went by. The two young men were introduced to us at church, and during our church social, we became better acquainted. Later on, Phillip asked permission to date my sister, Rachel. We started the new school year. On our way home from school one day we were hitchhiking. The school was four miles from town. We got a ride in a pick-up truck with a camper. A few minutes later the truck stopped and picked up Phillip and Herman also. They sat across from us in the camper just staring at us.

Later on, Phillip brought Herman by our home to visit and made several visits bringing coconuts and fruits for me. Herman asked my mom permission to date me. I was upset because he did not ask me first. I told my mom I was not sure I wanted to date him. She told me to pray about it, so that night I prayed. The next day I was not happy, because I needed a sign from God. I told Mom I needed a sign, and she told me to pray for a sign. I recalled the story in the Bible about Gideon praying for a sign. It was the rainy season, that night it was raining very heavily, and the weather report said it would rain for several days.

That night with the rain beating down on our roof I prayed that it would be sunny and dry the next day. We all went to bed. The next morning I woke up to no rain, there was no rain clouds in the sky; instead, it was blue sky and sunny. I then said, "To be this way, the weatherman made a mistake!" That night I listened to the weather report for the next day, and it was expected to be sunny and dry. There was a break in the weather, so I prayed to God for it to be raining and thundering and a heavy downpour if Herman was to be my boyfriend. I asked God for the contrary.

The next day we woke up to thundering and lightning, the day was overcast with dark clouds all over the sky, and heavy rain. I said the weatherman didn't know what he was talking about. I checked the weather forecast for the third day, and it was to rain again. I prayed for God to make the opposite, and it was beautiful and dry.

The sun was shining, the skies were blue, so I said, "I won't pray that prayer anymore."

It was not working. After family worship each evening, Mom would always spray for mosquitoes before we went to bed, but this night she did not spray. This was the fourth night.

Before I lay down, I prayed to God since Mom did not spray. I said if Herman is the one for me, let there be a dead roach at the foot of my bed the next morning. I was terrified of roaches. In my mind that was impossible for God. When I awoke the next morning, to my amazement there was three dead roaches belly up in front of my bed.

I screamed, "Mom! Mom! You spray last night!"

"Girl, you know I would not spray that poison over you all while sleeping."

I then told Mom all about the past three nights I had prayed for signs, and the fourth night I prayed for a dead roach to show up, but now there were three dead roaches instead. What was the meaning of three dead roaches? Mom said the three roaches were the three nights that I prayed and did not believe God.

That is when I knew that he was the one for me. We started dating and three years later on August 14 at 5:00 p.m. we were married at the 54th Street SDA Church in Los Angeles, California. Thirty-four years later we are still together. When contemplating about a spouse one should earnestly seek God's approval, and He will guide you in finding the right one.

We invite you to view the complete
selection of titles we publish at:
www.TEACHServices.com

We encourage you to write us
with your thoughts about this,
or any other book we publish at:
info@TEACHServices.com

TEACH Services' titles may be purchased in
bulk quantities for educational, fund-raising,
business, or promotional use.
bulksales@TEACHServices.com

Finally, if you are interested in seeing
your own book in print, please contact us at:
publishing@TEACHServices.com
We are happy to review your manuscript at no charge.

www.ingramcontent.com/pod-product-compliance
Lightning Source LLC
Chambersburg PA
CBHW061414090426
42742CB00023B/3468